# REACH *THE* FOUNTAIN *OF* YOUTH

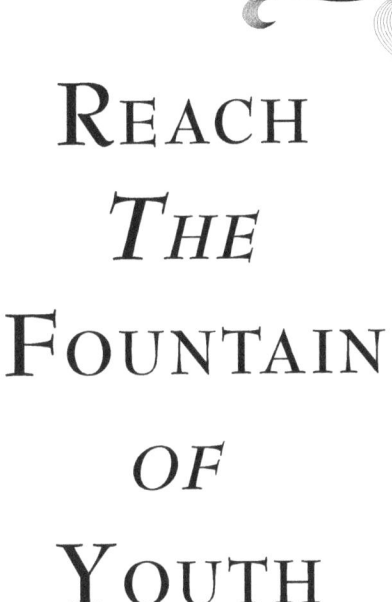

## Also by Torry Fountinhead

*The 7 Pillars Your Authentic Self Stands On*, Part I of *The Essential Companion Series*

*The Beauty*, Part I of *The Contemplation Series*

*The Soul's Openner – Enchanting The Soul to 'Being'*

Part II of *The Contemplation Series*

*Shush! It's a Secret, The Lake Hides His Dummy*, Part of *The Rainbow of Life's Secrets*

*Poem: Good Enough*, Part of *Forever Spoken, The International Library of Poetry*

*A Tip of an Iceberg Meditations*, a series of short books (see the series' list at http://atipofanicebergmeditations.ca)

and many more at work…

# Reach The Fountain of Youth

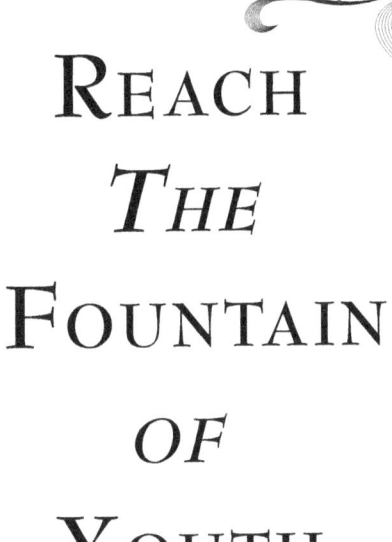

Part III of "Contemplations" Series

By

Torry Fountinhead

Airé Libré Publishing & Computing Ltd.

**Print Book ISBNs:**
ISBN-10: 0-9808964-2-8
ISBN-13: 978-0-9808964-2-8

© **2018 Torry Fountinhead**
All Rights of this work are Reserved. No part or whole may be used, copied or reproduced, stored in retrieval systems, or transmitted, in any form or by any means whatsoever, including electronic media, mechanical, photocopying, recording, or otherwise.

For more information contact:
Airé Libré Publishing & Computing Ltd.
Suite 306, 185-911 Yates St.
Victoria BC V8V 4Y9 Canada
Tel: 1-250-592-3099.
http://www.al.bc.ca   info@al.bc.ca

***Book Web-Site URLs:***
http://reachthefountainofyouth.torryfountinhead.ca

***Part of:***
**Http://contemplations.al.bc.ca**

# REACH *THE* FOUNTAIN *OF* YOUTH

## *Prologue*

"People, both young and old, simple and experts, throughout the centuries, were seeking The Fountain of Youth not wanting to accept, what seemed to be, the destiny of each one. Legends were created, but no answer at hand. What if we have had the answer in the palm of our hands - ALL THE TIME."

Contemplations are our tool to go within, to reach the wisdom of the ages, as we connect to Universal Mind. It does have some requirements though, so read on, and reach to it.

*Reach The Fountain of Youth*

# Love Life

*Reach The Fountain of Youth*

# Embrace & Bask in Joy

*Reach The Fountain of Youth*

# Think of Better days

# Remember, The Sun Is Still Shining Behind The Clouds

*Reach The Fountain of Youth*

# Look For The Flowers

*Reach The Fountain of Youth*

# Smell The Flowers

*Reach The Fountain of Youth*

# Smell The Coffee If There Aren't Any Flowers

*Reach The Fountain of Youth*

# Be There, Be Surprised & Laugh

*Reach The Fountain of Youth*

# Raise Your Head Even Though Your Neck Is Sore

*Reach The Fountain of Youth*

# Remember, Pain Is Only A Messenger, Listen In

# Be Young At Heart
## After all, Your Soul Is Eternal and Thus, Does Not Age, And Your Body Regenerate Fully In Less Than 7 Years, So *You Are* Young

*Reach The Fountain of Youth*

# Choose The Path of Joy, Let Go Of The Path Of Struggle

# The Wave Of Life, The Ups & Downs, Is The Way To Take You To Dance

# What Goes Down, Must Come Up, We're Not Made To Remain Down, We're Forever Growing

# Evolving, Growing, Progressing, And Developing Is The Way Of Nature

*Reach The Fountain of Youth*

# Look At The Streams Of Joy Flowing From The Eyes Of A Laughing Baby

# Listen To The Streams Of Joy Flowing Through A Baby's Laughter

*Reach The Fountain of Youth*

# Let Music Evoke Deep Feelings Within You

# When Choosing Good Music, Do So To Promote Your Growth

*Reach The Fountain of Youth*

# Listen To The Gift
# A Singer Gives You
# With Their Full Heart

# Beauty Is All Around You, As It Is In The Eye Of The Beholder Be A Good Beholder!

*Reach The Fountain of Youth*

# Assume There Is Beauty In Everything

# Beauty Not Seen Is Beauty That Hasn't Been Discovered As Yet

# Temporary Beauty Reminds Us Of Every Moment's Preciousness

# Fleeting Happiness Is Still Happiness

*Reach The Fountain of Youth*

# Practice Feeling Happiness

*Reach The Fountain of Youth*

# Wiggle Your Toes, If You Have None, Do It In Your Imagination

# Breathe In Again, Deeply, Feel The Gift Of 'Being'

*Reach The Fountain of Youth*

# Within Your Mind Imagine Dancing, It Will Set You Free

*Reach The Fountain of Youth*

# Move Your Body, Fasten Your Circulation, It Will Help You Feel Alive

# Shake Off Unwanted Thoughts – You Are Not Your Thoughts Anyway

*Reach The Fountain of Youth*

# Assume There Is Goodness In Everything

*Reach The Fountain of Youth*

# Look For Goodness, And You'll Find It

# Thank Your Feelings, And Remember, You Are Not Your Feelings

*Reach The Fountain of Youth*

# Think Of Your Feelings As A Song Played On The Strings Of Your Heart

# If You Don't Like The Song, Look At An Uplifting Sight

# When You Look, Do It Either With Your Physical Eyes, Or With Your Mind Eyes

# No One Can Take Your Mind Away From You – Use It Well

# Think Of Your Mind As The Soil Of Your Private Garden

# Grow Beautiful Fruit Trees & Flowers In Your Private Garden

*Reach The Fountain of Youth*

# Enjoy Your Beautiful Private Garden

*Reach The Fountain of Youth*

# Make Your Private Garden Your 'Safe' Place

# Take Frequent Breaks, And Visit Your 'Safe' Place

# In Your Imagination, Every Cloudy Day Can Be Changed To A Sunny One

# If You Feel Constricted, Take A Deep Breath Again

*Reach The Fountain of Youth*

# Remember That This Too Shall Pass

# Dance Your Feelings Away, Make Space For The New

*Reach The Fountain of Youth*

# When You Say Goodbye To The Unwanted, You Are Already Welcoming The Wanted

# Like Pain, The Unwanted Had A Message, Receive It & Move On

*Reach The Fountain of Youth*

# Let Go Gently & Smoothly, And Not In Desperation

*Reach The Fountain of Youth*

# The New Takes Time To Settle In, Have Patience

# Patience Is Like Watching A Flower Bloom

# Check In To See If You're Hibernating, You Might Emerge As A Beautiful Butterfly

# If You Happen To Procrastinate, Imagine What Might You Lose Because Of It

# If You're In A Hurry, Imagine How Much You've Missed In Your Rush

# Remember, 'All In Good Time', And Breathe Deeply Again

# Remember, You Can Only Control Yourself

# Controlling Others?! That's An Illusion & Delusion

# When You Criticise Another, You Say: 'I Want To Control You'

*Reach The Fountain of Youth*

# Remain Free, Cease Giving Or Receiving Criticism

# Freedom Allows You To be & Become Your Authentic Self

# Following Your Own True Path Is In line With Being Authentic

Allowing Others
To Follow
Their Own Path,
Frees You From
Responsibility
For Their Happiness

*Reach The Fountain of Youth*

# We Travel Though The Birth Canal One By One, Live & Let Live

# Be Supportive, Remember You Were Supported Right From The Moment Of Your Conception

*Reach The Fountain of Youth*

# Your Essence Is Joy, So Smile

# A Smile Positively Affects Your Whole Physiology, Do It Often

# When You Don't Find It In You, Make A Cup Of Tea, And Relax

# A Tea Ceremony Is Actually A Relaxing Ritual, Enjoy It

# Emotions In Turmoil? Bring Yourself From The Outer Storm, To The Eye Of The Storm, Where All Is Calm

# Emotions Are Energy In Motion, Use This Energy Positively When Releasing It

# The Emotions Energy Is Yours, Why Waste It?

*Reach The Fountain of Youth*

# You're The One Giving Your Emotions Their Colour & Taste, Choose Well

# Your Emotions Are Yours To Hold, Or Let Go, Welcoming Others

*Reach The Fountain of Youth*

# Youth In Its Heart Is Innocence & Joy, Don't Destroy It

# Innocence, And Even Naiveté, Is Not Ignorance, It Is Pure

# Never Feel Less Than Another, You Are Created Perfect

*Reach The Fountain of Youth*

# Never Feel More Than Another, They Are Created Perfect

# Opinions Are Ever Moving Like The Wind

# Don't Let The Wind Of Opinions Be A Destructive Hurricane

*Reach The Fountain of Youth*

# Choose To Be Light As A Pleasant & Gentle Day's Breeze

*Reach The Fountain of Youth*

# A Child Looks For Recognition, Appreciation, Encouragement, And Love
# Treat Yourself Well

# See
# The Loveable Child
# In Everyone Else

*Reach The Fountain of Youth*

# The Gold That Is In Your Heart Was Forged From Source

*Reach The Fountain of Youth*

# The Same Gold Is In All Hearts, As They Were Forged From The Same Source

# Being Youthful Is Being Alive Within The Rhythm Of Life

# Remaining Youthful Means That You Adhere To The Rhythm Of Life

# The Fountain Of Youth Is Your Innate Ability To Adjust To The Rhythm Of Life

# Why Let Anything, Or Anyone, Rob You Of Your Flow?

*Reach The Fountain of Youth*

# Why Would You Rob Anything, Or Anyone, Of Their Flow?

Remember, The Free
Things In Life Are
Free For A Reason
They Are There To
Nourish You
Regardless

*Reach The Fountain of Youth*

# Love, Joy, Happiness, And The Like Are Independent Of Price, And Yet Priceless

# Beauty, Goodness, Goodwill, And Abundance Surround You, Bask In Them

*Reach The Fountain of Youth*

# You Do What You Want To Do, So Do That Which Promotes You

# You Don't Do What You Don't Want To Do, So Stay Away From Any Harm

*Reach The Fountain of Youth*

# Remember That The Skies Are Blue Behind The Clouds

*Reach The Fountain of Youth*

# On A Rainy Day, Remember, Nature Is Cleansing All

# Remember That Your Tears Cleanse You

# After Crying, Say To Yourself: 'Good Job', And Smile

*Reach The Fountain of Youth*

# Never Say Good-bye
# Say *Adieu*

## *Epilogue*

Now that you have journeyed through the profound sayings that meant to ignite in you the spark of Life, I would like to say something more.

I could have brought you mountains of studies, in many sciences and modalities that might have satisfied your analytical reasoning. A data such that may justify this day and age way of thinking, because it can speak of hormone generation, nervous influence, health implications, etc. etc. etc.

Do you need it?

Don't you actually need the proof 'in the field?'

If you walk down the street with your head held high, spring in your step, smile on your face, because you 'just' enjoy Life, and thus, you, and people notice you, and you get varied responses – isn't it saying 'you are alive, you do exist, you are intriguing'?

The fountain of youth is held close to you, within you, and when you allow it to flow – this is what would happen.

Shell off your coats of disbelief, doubts, common beliefs in doom and gloom and aging. Shell them off, become innocent like a babe who 'knows' that it is being taking care of by All Life.

Be courageous and strong, and walk tall. Fill your heart with Joy, and collect the dew drops of Happiness, every day shall pass too, whether good or bad – you are safe and sound.

Be rooted in the assurance of your value, and the right to live well.

Love is in the air…

Be Well.

www.ingramcontent.com/pod-product-compliance
Lightning Source LLC
Chambersburg PA
CBHW031407160426
43196CB00007B/931